Original title:
Tales of the Timber Trail

Copyright © 2025 Creative Arts Management OÜ
All rights reserved.

Author: Maxwell Donovan
ISBN HARDBACK: 978-1-80567-428-3
ISBN PAPERBACK: 978-1-80567-727-7

The Quiet Grace of Greenery

In the woods where chatter grows,
A squirrel steals snacks, he knows.
With acorns tucked, he makes a dash,
While branches creak, the leaves all clash.

Uncle Owl's asleep on high,
While Robin sings a silly cry.
A chipmunk looks, all big and bright,
As if confused by morning light.

From Canopy to Clearing

Through leaves I see a funny sight,
A raccoon prancing left and right.
It stumbled once, then twice, then more,
With borrowed shoes from a gusty bore.

The bumbles in the flower beds,
Tell all the secrets, like they're bred.
The bees are buzzing, what a dance!
It's clear they've joined the fray by chance.

The Everlasting Echo

In the forest, echoes play,
A tree stump laughs the day away.
The echo thinks it's quite the brat,
Chasing sounds like a playful cat.

A bear comes by with berry stains,
While singing loud—his tethered chains.
"Stop that racket!" an old deer shouts,
Smiling wide, he knows the route.

The Spirit of the Woodland Wanderer

The wanderer trips on roots and stones,
With joyous laughter, he groans and moans.
The map in hand, he squints at trees,
While squirrels giggle in the breeze.

A light-footed fox joins in the fun,
Chasing shadows, always on the run.
Each stumble bounces with a smile,
A woodland party, they stay awhile.

A Tapestry of Twisted Branches

In a wood where branches twist,
A squirrel plays with light,
He thinks he's quite the daredevil,
Nutty antics take flight.

A raccoon dons a fancy hat,
Stealing snacks with glee,
He winks at all the birds above,
"You can't catch me!" he brags.

The Enigma of the Elderwood

An old tree stands with a knowing grin,
Whispers secrets of yore,
While caterpillars dance in a line,
On leaves that start to bore.

A chipmunk plays detective,
Searching for lost acorns,
He checks behind the mushrooms,
And finds two rubber horns!

Serenade of the Silent Stream

A stream that babbles soft and sweet,
Sings a tune so bright,
It tickles frogs beneath the reeds,
Who hop with pure delight.

A fish with dreams of fame and stage,
Winks at ducks in flight,
"One day I'll swim on Broadway,
Just watch my talents ignite!"

Revelations from the Rustic Road

On a winding path where the wildflowers bloom,
A goat thinks it's a car,
He tries to steer with mighty hooves,
But just goes too far!

The rabbit is the traffic cop,
With ears that stand so tall,
He giggles as he waves them through,
"Just drive and have a ball!"

Beneath the Boughs of Time

In a forest deep, where squirrels play,
They thought they'd race, but lost their way.
A rabbit chuckled, with a twitching nose,
While a snail proudly flaunted its glows.

A tree stump grumbled, 'times are a-changin',
Complaining of kids who just keep rearrangin'.
A woodpecker laughed from its perch so high,
As moths danced near, under the clear blue sky.

Vignettes from the Verdant Valley

In a meadow bright, a goat wore a hat,
He claimed it was chic, but we knew it was fat.
The ducks quacked loud, in a fashion debate,
While a hedgehog rolled by, completely irate.

A pair of raccoons tried their best to dance,
But tripped on a log, missing their chance.
The bumblebees buzzed, spreading sweet cheer,
As a frog croaked loudly, 'Hey, look, I'm here!'

The Swaying Dance of Driftwood

On the riverbank, where the driftwood sways,
A fish told a tale of the clumsy days.
With flops and splashes, it splattered the scene,
While a beaver just chuckled, 'That's never been seen!'

A log rolled along, dancing a jig,
While a turtle just sighed, 'Oh, look at that pig.'
They spun and they twirled, all in good fun,
Under the warmth of the setting sun.

Parables of the Pinecones

Once heavy pinecones fell like the rain,
Landing on heads, causing laughter and pain.
A chipmunk declared, 'It's a pinecone parade!'
As the forest erupted, a joke was made.

A wise old owl hooted, 'Listen up, friends,'
'The laughter we share is what truly transcends.'
As sunlight flickered through branches that sway,
The pinecones still giggled, all throughout the day.

The Echoing Silence of Trees

In the forest so deep, where the odd critters creep,
Whispers bounce back, making squirrels lose sleep.
A raccoon once shouted, 'I'm not a raccoon!',
The trees giggled softly, in tune with the moon.

Branches wore glasses, their style was unique,
Tree trunks bowed proudly, they practiced to speak.
One said to a pine, 'You look quite a fright!',
But the pine just chuckled, 'I'm right here, alright!'

Mysteries of the Mossy Glen

In a glen thick with moss, where the mushrooms do dance,

Lived a frog with a crown, who fancied romance.
He croaked to a lady, 'What say you, my dear?',
She replied, 'Only if you can hop without fear!'

Along came a rabbit with an ear so grand,
He whispered a riddle as he shook his hand.
'What's small and has hops, but can't make a meal?'
The frog scratched his head, 'Is it me or a wheel?'

Chronicles of the Whispering Winds

The wind told me tales of a kite in a thrum,
That soared with a seagull, both looking quite dumb.
They twisted and turned in a great swirling dance,
While a nearby old tree just laughed at their chance.

'What's life without rumbles of laughter and cheer?'
The leaves cheered in chorus, 'Just keep us all near!'
The breeze blew a tune that made everyone sway,
So kites tickled seagulls until the end of day.

Adventures Along the Twisting Trail

On a trail that was winding, where no one could pause,
A tortoise named Timmy lost sight of his cause.
He met a fast rabbit, who winked with a grin,
'You're slow as molasses, but I'll share my spin!'

They raced side by side, though Timmy took naps,
The rabbit hummed tunes, while Timmy just flaps.
When they reached the end, both smiled with delight,
'The journey was grand, and who cares about right?'

Whispers of the Wooded Way

In the shadow of the trees,
A squirrel lost his keys.
He searched among the leaves,
And giggled at the bees.

A raccoon wore a hat,
Thought he was quite the cat.
He danced a little jig,
While chasing down a rat.

The owls threw a big party,
With snacks that looked quite hearty.
But when the moon grew bright,
They all turned a bit farty.

The foxes played charades,
In masks made from cascade.
But all the songs they sung,
Left the frogs feeling betrayed.

The Journey of Root and Wing

A parrot found a boot,
Thought it would make a suit.
He strutted up the path,
And ended up in loot.

A turtle chased a hare,
Through thickets, unaware.
He tripped over a log,
And ended up in air.

The bees threw a parade,
But who forgot the shade?
They fluttered all around,
Too much nectar, I'm afraid!

A deer sang in the sun,
Each note more out of fun.
The grasshoppers all cheered,
And then they all did run.

Song of the Solitary Spruce

A lonely spruce stood tall,
With ornaments in thrall.
The forest critters laughed,
As snow fell with a sprawl.

A chipmunk took a call,
From squirrels, one and all.
They planned a nutty feast,
And issues did befall.

The wind began to tease,
With whispers through the trees.
"Call me spruces' friend,"
Squeaked the squirrels with ease.

The roots all started to groove,
And the canopy made a move.
In this whimsical ballet,
All nature found its groove.

Fables from the Forest Floor

In hammocks made of vines,
A sloth read ancient signs.
But every sleepy yawn,
Brought giggles from the pines.

A snail won a race,
And took it slow with grace.
The rabbits thought it funny,
"Who needs a fast-paced place?"

The sun began to rise,
With colors in the skies.
All critters danced around,
While trying not to fry.

So if you're in the woods,
And laughter is the goods,
Join in with all the fun,
Among the chirps and hoods.

Treading on Timber Tales

A squirrel hoards acorns like gold,
He thinks he's the king, proud and bold.
But when winter comes, he finds to his dismay,
He forgot where he hid them, oh what a day!

The rabbit hops fast, with laughter and glee,
Until he trips over roots, oh whee, oh me!
He lands in a puddle, splashed all around,
Now he's the wettest bunny in town!

A deer snickers softly at a mouse's dance,
The mouse trips and falls, it was quite the chance.
Yet up he gets, with a dazzling twirl,
And they all burst with laughter, watch that little swirl!

The old wise owl, perched high on a tree,
Wonders why they don't take life seriously.
But his chuckle erupts, he can't help but grin,
A forest of laughter, let the fun begin!

A Journey Through Padded Pathways

Down the path where the soft moss grows,
A hedgehog rolls by, striking silly poses.
He thought it quite clever to journey along,
Until he rolled over and sang a wrong song!

A snail on a stroll takes his time, oh true,
With a shell like a house, his pace is askew.
But when he meets friends, they laugh and they scurry,
Dashing past puddles, oh what a flurry!

Frogs leap in rhythm, a wobbly dance,
With lily pad shoes, they take a chance.
Yet one little frog, slips right on his rear,
And the rest burst with laughter, their giggles sincere!

As they rush back home, after fun to impart,
Each creature chuckles, filled with joy at heart.
With padded pathways beneath their furry feet,
They'll share their adventures, oh, what a treat!

Glades of Solitude

In a quiet glade, where breezes hum,
A tortoise thinks, 'I'm really quite dumb!'
He tries to dance, in the evening light,
But trips on a log, oh what a sight!

A lonely wildcat practices his pounce,
But a branch snaps, and he starts to bounce.
He gets tangled up, his fur in a mess,
What was a sneak feels more like excess!

There under the trees, owl shares a grin,
At the antics that he cannot begin.
"Why rush?" he hoots, "Life's more like a song,"
And with that, he joins, both dancing along!

In glades so serene, the laughter will flow,
Echoing softly, where wild breezes blow.
Each creature's a friend, though solitude reigns,
In these funny moments, nothing remains plain!

The Chronicle of the Crafting Creatures

An ant with a hammer builds homes with flare,
But each nail he pounds, he's lost in despair.
For the wood is too thick, the roof's gone astray,
Looks like his plans have all gone away!

A beaver so clever, with branches aplenty,
Starts crafting a dam; optimism's entry.
Yet end of the day, it's awash with a twirl,
And instead of a dam, he's built a whirlpool!

A bumblebee buzzes with crafting delight,
Creating a vase that's a wonderful sight.
But it tips and it spills, oh the honey, oh dear!
Now he's dripped sweet gold flowing everywhere here!

The forest alights with laughter and cheer,
As critters join in, no need to disappear.
For in chronicles funny, where crafting holds sway,
Life's mishaps make music; let's dance and play!

Moonlit Memories of the Trail

Under the stars we tripped and fell,
Laughter echoed like a jolly bell.
A raccoon stole our midnight snack,
We chased him down, but he was too quick back!

The owls hooted, 'Keep the noise down!',
While our jokes made the whole woodland frown.
With bushes tickling our silly sides,
We danced like fools, with no place to hide!

A splash from the stream made us scream,
It was just a frog, living its dream.
Belly laughs echoed through the night,
As shadows waltzed in the moonlight!

Home we strolled, with giggles in tow,
Under the moon's soft, silvery glow.
These nights of joy, we'll always keep,
Chasing shadows before we sleep!

A Tapestry of Twisting Vines

In the jungle gym of green delight,
Vines twisted 'round, a wild sight.
We swung and twirled like crazy bees,
    Bumping into trees with ease!

A monkey watched with a cheeky grin,
    As we attempted a victory spin.
One fall, two falls, we tumbled down,
Sending leaves flying all over town!

Chasing butterflies, we lost our way,
Through the wild maze, we'd laugh and play.
Who knew vines could lead to such fun?
Our adventure here had only begun!

With each laugh, the forest cheered,
For nature's joy is always revered.
So here we stay, wild and free,
Wrapped in laughter, just you and me!

The Call of the Wild Wanderer

Under the sun, with a hat so big,
The wild wanderer did a funny jig.
His compass spun, lost as could be,
But he danced on, full of glee!

A bear poked its head, oh what a sight,
Joining in, what a silly night!
They spun in circles, paws in the air,
What's a forest without a dance pair?

A squirrel jumped in, with nuts galore,
'What's a party without a snack score?'
They munched and munched, shared laughs so bright,
In this wild haven, all felt just right!

With giggles galore in the wild so vast,
Each step they took, a memory cast.
For laughter echoes through the tall trees,
In the heart of nature, life's greatest tease!

Chronicles of Canopy Creatures

In the canopy, where critters meet,
A parrot squawked, 'This can't be beat!'
With every sound, a tale unfurled,
Of jungle antics in a wacky world!

A sloth tripped down from a lofty branch,
Said, 'Oh dear! I'll take a chance!'
He crashed on a raccoon's hidden stash,
Turns out, that's how they made a splash!

The frogs croaked out beatbox tunes,
While fireflies danced in shimmering swoons.
The party grew louder, with giggles abound,
As critters from every nook came around!

With stories shared of mishaps and glee,
In the wildest of times, joy is key.
These chronicles of laughter unite,
In the heart of the forest, all feels right!

Shadows Dancing on Sunlit Trails

Beneath the trees, shadows play,
Squirrels dance in a cheeky way.
A rabbit trips over a funny stone,
And the breeze whispers, 'You're not alone.'

The sun shines bright, the leaves do sway,
A chipmunk laughs, then runs away.
The ants are marching, all in line,
While the owls hoot jokes at half-past nine.

A bear in shades takes a sunlit nap,
Dreaming of honey and a cozy lap.
A raccoon juggles acorns with flair,
As the winds carry laughter through the air.

On this trail, laughter's the rule,
Every creature plays the fool.
In the forest's warmth, let joy prevail,
Come join the fun on this bright trail.

The Enchanted Expedition

Packed up tight with snacks to munch,
We set out on our little hunch.
A frog hops by with a witty quip,
While a toadstool teases, 'Take a dip!'

Through the thicket, we stumble and fall,
Chasing after a butterfly ball.
A squirrel winks, then darts away,
Leading us on with a playful sway.

We met a fox who read our fate,
He grinned and claimed, 'It's rather late!'
But with magic tricks up his fur sleeve,
He made us chuckle, we couldn't believe!

With every twist, we found delight,
In hidden treasures and silly sights.
So here we roam, pure and free,
On this expedition for you and me.

Chronicle of the Cone and the Fern

A cunning cone rolled from the tree,
Declaring, 'Come laugh, it's fun, you'll see!'
A fern replied with a swaying dance,
'Let's spin around and take a chance!'

The wind blew wild, they tumbled fast,
Into the brook with a splash and a blast.
The fish giggled as they swirled by,
While the clouds above waved good-bye.

They held a contest, who'd stay dry,
The cone won, but the fern flew high.
With sprigs and giggles, they twirled around,
Creating laughter in every sound.

Together they ventured, side by side,
In the laughter of nature, they did glide.
A friendship blooming in fun and cheers,
The cone and the fern, spreading joy for years!

Ramblings Through the Rustic Realm

Through fields of flowers, we wander wide,
A goat in glasses, my trusty guide.
He points and says, 'Now look right there,
A cow's wearing a hat, with style and flair!'

With every step, adventures unfold,
We meet woodland critters, brave and bold.
A hedgehog sings with a voice so shrill,
While the trees chuckle at his odd little thrill.

A picnic awaits by the babbling brook,
With sandwiches shaped like a curious book.
A raccoon swipes fries with a cheeky grin,
As the sun sets low, let the fun begin!

In this rustic realm, laughter is king,
With silly happenings that make hearts sing.
So join the dance in the golden light,
Where every moment feels just right!

Flickering Lights Among the Firs

Beneath the pines, a glow so bright,
A raccoon dances, what a sight!
He wears a hat that's way too small,
And trips on roots as he starts to fall.

The squirrels chuckle, oh what a show,
As he wiggles and jigs in the moonlight's glow.
With nuts in hand, they cheer him on,
While he twirls around till the break of dawn.

Murmurs in the Misty Grove

In the fog, a whisper grows loud,
A bear is singing, feeling proud.
He thinks he's smooth, his voice like silk,
But sounds more like a cow's milked milk.

Nearby, the owls roll their big eyes,
Wondering how he thinks he'll win the prize.
With each off-key note, the trees just sway,
While foxes laugh and run away.

Paths of the Veiled Canopy

A rabbit races down a path,
Chasing shadows, but what a laugh!
He darts past trees with his big ears flopping,
Tripping on roots, bellyaches stopping.

Suddenly, he stumbles into a stream,
With a sploosh and a splash, oh what a dream!
Fish tease him, flipping with a grin,
While he shakes off water, ready to win.

Songbirds and Hidden Glades

The birds decide to hold a band,
Each one strumming with a crazy hand.
A chicken joins, awkward yet proud,
While the sparrows giggle, forming a crowd.

With wormy solos and chirpy backup,
They rattle the leaves, but never give up.
The tree trunks shudder, a dance begins,
As nature cheers at their silly wins.

The Beneath of Boughs

In the grove where squirrels prance,
A rabbit's caught in a chipmunk's dance.
With acorns spinning like a top,
Laughter echoes, never stop!

Under branches, shadows play,
Frogs wear crowns in a wacky way.
A bear tries yoga, oh so bold,
While a wise old owl shares tales of old.

The pinecones drop like silly hats,
While raccoons plan their midnight chats.
Each creature's antics bring delight,
In the wood's grand, goofy night!

With every rustle, giggles grow,
As deer join in on the show.
Nature's circus, wild and free,
Where every laugh is a jubilee!

The Story Weaved in Tree Rings

In rings of wood, secrets peek,
A chipmunk shares his weekly streak.
Oh, the gossip these trees could tell,
In whispers soft, they know it well.

A squirrel's tale, a twisty fate,
He thinks he's stealthy; oh, but wait!
The pinecone's hit, and down he goes,
Landing softly in a bed of rose.

Leaves swirl like dancers in the fall,
While squirrels invite us, one and all.
They tease and chase, a comical sight,
Nature's stage is pure delight!

From those old rings, with humor rare,
The forest laughs, with charm to spare.
Each bark a chuckle, every trunk a joke,
In the merry wood, no one's ever broke!

The Hidden Heart of the Forest

Deep in the woods, where giggles hide,
A fox pursues a butterfly glide.
With every dash and playful chase,
They twirl and spin in a charming race.

A bear in pajamas, oh what a sight,
Cuddles trees while dreaming at night.
Raccoons wear masks, look quite absurd,
As they plot mischief, not a word heard.

Woodpeckers drum in a silly beat,
While ants march off to their own retreat.
Each nook and cranny holds a jest,
In nature's heart, there's fun at best!

With foliage thick, the laughter swells,
Among the ferns, the forest dwells.
Where every creature plays a role,
In this woodland show, joy takes its toll!

Beneath the Canopy's Cover

Under the arch where shadows meet,
A raccoon taps with two tiny feet.
He jokes with a hedgehog, puffed with pride,
While caterpillars laugh, side by side.

Frogs croak out their songs so weird,
While a ladybug's dance leaves us cheered.
The laughter tumbles like leaves that fall,
Beneath the canopy, joy's a free call!

A twirling squirrel takes to the air,
As nutty antics fill the fair.
With chattering birds that whistle low,
Nature's comedy, the best show!

In this realm of green delight,
Where jokes and jests take off in flight.
Under the boughs, pure fun we find,
A quirk-filled world, sweetly designed!

The Restless Spirits of the Thicket

In a tangle of branches, they giggle and sway,
Spirits that dance, they've come out to play.
With a rustle of leaves, they pull off their tricks,
Scaring the birds, giving squirrels a fix.

A branch slips, a twig cracks, they all start to quake,
The owls roll their eyes at the mess that they make.
Chasing the shadows as daylight drifts by,
These naughty old phantoms just live to comply.

With laughter and echoes, they weave through the pines,
Crafting their mischief, blurring the lines.
When the moon rises up, they organize pranks,
Mixing up acorns and changing the ranks.

So if you should wander through woods old and spry,
Listen for giggles and give it a try.
For in the thicket, beneath the green cloak,
Restless spirits are jiving—who could be broke?

Dreams Woven in Bark

In the heart of the forest, dreams twine and loop,
Bark whispers stories in its ancient scoop.
With every soft rustle, a giggle emits,
As critters debate on who tells the wits.

A squirrel with a hat, declaring he's king,
Tells the trees tales of the joys that they bring.
The raccoons chortle, they couldn't agree,
Who bestows wisdom from trunk to the bee.

A nightingale chirps in a lopsided tone,
Proclaiming the seed of a mythical stone.
But the bark just chuckles, its grooves full of fun,
Saying, "Join in the dance, for the night's just begun!"

So whirl with the dreams that are sprouting so wide,
In the laughter of branches, let humor abide.
For the forests' comedic skits don't need spark,
Just a sprinkle of giggles and dreams woven in bark.

The Brush of Winds and Whispers

Whispers flutter by as the breezes all laugh,
Gathering gossip, they're quick to craft.
With playful nudges, they tickle the leaves,
Spreading the word of the tossing thieves.

Squirrels chat chattering, so full of delight,
As branches entwine in a frolicking fight.
"Who stole the acorns?" they holler with glee,
"For I found a stash and it's not just for me!"

The winds weave a tale, like a riddle in flight,
Swirling and twirling, they follow the night.
Echoing laughter from nooks far and wide,
While the moon plays along, a cheeky old guide.

So take to the pathways where whispers take wing,
Let laughter flow loosely and begin to swing.
For the brush of the winds, with secrets to share,
Holds the charm of the forest—a whimsical fare!

Trails of Echoes and Embers

Embarking on trails where the echoes abound,
The twigs crackle softly, a mischievous sound.
Chasing after shadows, the giggles run wild,
Like a playful ghost, nature's own little child.

Around every corner, the embers ignite,
As animals gather, their spirits so bright.
A firefly's wink sends the frogs in a spree,
Croaking the jokes, as laughter's decree.

Pine needles giggle beneath pattering feet,
As branches lean close to eavesdrop on heat.
The stories unfold in a whirlwind of cheer,
With echoes of laughter, they ring crystal clear.

So, wander the pathways of mischief and song,
Join in the fun, where the wild get along!
For trails will remember the joy that it sends,
With the echoes and embers, let humor transcend.

An Odyssey of Oak and Ash

Deep in the woods, where the squirrels play,
A raccoon once tried to save the day.
He wore a top hat, quite regal and grand,
And danced on the logs like a rock band!

A wise old owl gave a hoot to the crowd,
"This party's the best, let's all laugh loud!"
But a bear in a tutu stole all the snacks,
Creating a mess, oh what fun it lacks!

They planned a parade down the leaf-laden lane,
With pinecone trumpets, they made a strange gain.
The rabbits all leapt to a bizarre tune,
While the deer played the drums by the light of the moon.

As twilight descended, the creatures got tired,
From dancing and laughter, their joy had fired.
With a final goodnight, they snuggled in close,
And vowed to return for more fun the most!

Glistening Reflections on the Riverbank

At the riverbank where the critters convene,
A frog donned a crown, a fanciful scene.
He croaked out a tune, quite flat but sincere,
While fish flipped their tails in a splashy cheer!

A turtle named Timmy, slow as a slug,
Decided to race a jittery bug.
With a wiggle and jiggle, it zipped right on by,
Poor Timmy just smiled with a content sigh.

The sunflowers giggled with their heads in the breeze,
As a raccoon searched for his lost pair of keys.
"I left them right here, I swear on my tail!"
While a mouse snickered loudly, avoiding the trail.

Finally, the sun set on that chuckling shore,
With stories galore, they laughed 'til they snore.
From frogs in a crown to a turtle's missed goal,
The riverbank's memories filled every soul!

The Hollow's Hidden Heritage

In a hollow so deep, where the shadows all played,
Lived a woodpecker known for his colorful spade.
He drilled silly rhythms into the old trees,
While ladybugs gathered with giggles and glee!

A mystery brewed when a raccoon went mad,
He declared he'd discovered a treasure so rad!
But it was only an acorn, a prize from the past,
Which sparked a wild search that would surely last.

The owls rolled their eyes, giving knowing hoots,
As beavers all laughed, sporting their funny suits.
They held a warm feast with berries and pie,
While the old trees applauded with branches held high.

With laughter and joy echoing through the night,
The hollow's rich stories ignited delight.
In their quirky embrace, they shared a soft snore,
Hers, bursts of chuckles evermore!

Fables from the Forest Floor

On the forest floor where the mushrooms grow wide,
A crafty old fox threw a winkle-eyed slide.
The rabbits all hopped as he played with delight,
Crafting stories that sparkled under moonlight.

A vegan bear knuckle-bumped with a mouse,
While a snail in a top hat opened up house.
"Come join the fun, bring your finest dish!"
The woodland creatures squeaked, "Oh, what a wish!"

Their potluck was wild, with grubs and fine cheese,
As a turtle DJ played the rustling leaves.
They swayed and they twirled, in a merry ol' bash,
With fireflies voting for best dance - such a clash!

When the sun finally rose, they nestled in back,
Each critter was tired from their woodland attack.
With laughter in heart, they tucked in for the night,
In the forest so wild, everything felt just right!

A Ritual Beneath the Rustling Leaves

Beneath the branches green and wide,
The squirrels hold a treasure ride.
They stash acorns with great flair,
While raccoons plot their midnight dare.

The owls hoot jokes in quiet night,
As fireflies join in pure delight.
A picnic feast of berries sweet,
The forest's laugh, a lively treat.

With every twig a tale to tell,
The creatures grin, all is well.
In their own way, they dance and prance,
A silly, woodland, merry chance.

So let the trees bear witness true,
To critters bold in forest hue.
A gathering where fun's the key,
In rustling leaves, their jubilee.

Voices of the Verdant Voyage

Upon the path of green delight,
The frogs sing loudly, quite a sight.
They croak out songs of summer's cheer,
While turtles nod and swap a beer.

The chipmunks stage a grand parade,
With acorn hats, they're never frayed.
The rabbits laugh and hop in glee,
Embarking on a spree so free.

A parakeet with jokes so bright,
Makes every moment pure delight.
A leafy boat of giggles sail,
On waves of laughter through the vale.

In verdant nooks and sunlit glades,
The voices of the wild cascade.
A journey marked by silly plays,
In nature's arms, we spend our days.

Blossoms and Footprints

In fields where blooms and footprints roam,
The bees hold court, so far from home.
With pollen hats and dances grand,
They make their merry, buzzing band.

The flowers giggle, sway, and tease,
Embracing winds, the joyful breeze.
While butterflies in colors bright,
Chase laughter through the golden light.

Each bloom a story, sweet and fine,
Of playful blooms that twist and twine.
And in the dirt, a sock lies bare,
A lost little foot, but who would care?

The earth beneath keeps secrets close,
In blossoms' whispers, purest prose.
A tapestry of fun and cheer,
Where nature sings, our hearts will steer.

Solitudes of Sylvan Souls

In woodland realms where shadows play,
The fox discusses quirks of the day.
With a wink and a tail that sways,
He finds the oddest of ways to praise.

The deer share stories, tall and grand,
Of leaps and bounds across the land.
While moose take selfies, posing proud,
For social media, loud and loud.

The wise old owl, with glasses thick,
Reads from a book, performs a trick.
His audience, a raucous crew,
Laughing, hooting, all in view.

In sylvan nooks where secrets stir,
The laughter rises in a blur.
Among the trees, where silliness reigns,
A comedy of sorts flows through their veins.

Secrets of the Serene Summit

The turtle wore a silly hat,
And danced with glee, oh what of that!
A squirrel piped up with a joke or two,
While the mountain chuckled, 'What else is new?'

The birds teamed up for a comical show,
Singing wrong notes, oh what a blow!
With each little slip, they giggled more,
As the echoes bounced off the forest floor.

A rabbit joined in, juggling some stone,
But tripped on a root, and fell like a cone.
The laughter erupted, a joyous delight,
In the mystic heights, all seemed just right.

So secrets spun in the cool mountain air,
Of jests and blunders, beyond compare.
With whimsy and warmth, the day unfolded,
In the serene summit, humor enfolded.

Whispers Among the Pines

Under the pines, whispers grew loud,
As the chipmunks gathered, feeling so proud.
They shared all the fables of silly old Joe,
Who mistook a tree stump for his new buffalo!

The dapper old owl hooted with glee,
At the tales of the critters and their mischief spree.
So-a sassy old crow flapped his wings,
Poking fun at the raccoon who wore string!

The breeze brought laughter from ground to the sky,
As the flustered old fox gave a mighty sigh.
For every tall tale was sprinkled with cheer,
Among the tall pines where they gathered near.

So listen close when the winds begin to blow,
For secrets of laughter are in every flow.
In the heart of the woods, under the green vines,
Are the funny, sweet whispers among the pines.

Echoes of the Woodland Road

On the woodland road where the pathway winds,
Laughed a frog who twisted and squirmed, never minds.
He croaked out a rhythm, a silly old tune,
That made all the critters laugh under the moon!

A hedgehog with style, donned shades and a tie,
Swayed to the beat, offering up his sly eye.
The bees buzzed along with a choreographed buzz,
As a troupe of ants marched with humorous fuzz.

The trees leaned in closer to hear the great show,
While a snake attempted to limbo, oh woe!
He slipped on a pebble, with a twist and a flip,
And added to laughter with each clumsy trip.

So roam down this road where chuckles are found,
With echoes of joy all around and around.
For stories of fun and the mischief of old,
Fill the woodland road with laughter untold.

Journeys Through the Canopy

Through the canopy high, the monkeys do swing,
With capers and flips that make the woods ring.
One dropped his banana and shouted with flair,
While another burst out laughing, hanging in air!

The sloths, oh the sloths, took their sweet time,
Ignoring the antics with a languid chime.
As the vibrant parrots squawked out some remarks,
About the sloths' slow dance under the parks!

The branches were filled with chatter and cheer,
As the owls exchanged banter with each passing year.
A squirrel lost his footing, a tumble so grand,
But popped back up quick with the coolest of plans!

So journeys unfold where the laughter's set free,
In this leafy world, filled with glee.
From high-soaring antics to jokes on the breeze,
Through the canopy's heart, grownup giggles appease.

The Allure of the Ancient Arbor

In the shade of the old oak,
A squirrel stole my snack today.
It chattered while I blinked,
Then dashed quickly away.

The branches waved a hello,
As I tripped on a root.
The birds laughed at my tumble,
I'll get them back—whooot!

The breeze whispered secrets,
Of mushrooms with legs to dance.
I joined in their funny jig,
Completely lost my pants!

Oh, the ancient one chuckled,
As I tried to regain my pride.
With every slip and slide,
Life's a silly ride!

Lullabies of the Leafy Lull

Sleepy leaves dance softly,
While the crickets sing away.
The moon cracks a corny joke,
As night slips into play.

A chipmunk snores quite loudly,
In the hollow of a stump.
And whispers of the sweet dreams,
Make my sleepy heart thump.

Branches sway with laughter,
As shadows waltz away.
The night's a funny character,
In this leafy cabaret.

So close your eyes, dear forest,
With chuckles all around.
Rest well, my lively friends,
In joys, we're surely bound!

Myths of the Mossy Trailhead

At the mossy trailhead wandered,
A rabbit in a top hat.
He spun a yarn so silly,
I swear it made a cat!

With tales of dancing dandelions,
And frogs that wear nice shoes.
I laughed so hard I stumbled,
Tripped over my own blues.

A snail claimed he'd run a marathon,
But was napping at the line.
His friends all cheered and whispered,
'He's well-rested, feeling fine!'

Now whispers of the woodland,
Make even the trees snicker.
For deep in their green heart,
Lies humor that grows thicker!

The Oath of the Oakwood Brotherhood

Underneath the grandest elm,
We gathered for our pact.
To laugh through all our mischief,
And never fade to black.

A raccoon wore a crown of leaves,
Proclaiming himself our king.
With acorns as our treasures,
Oh, the joys this would bring!

We vowed to tickle the tallest trees,
And sing loud silly songs.
With every bough we bonked our heads,
We knew where we belonged.

So here's to oakwood brothers,
And all things light and free.
May laughter mark our tales,
In this old, enchanted spree!

Whispers of the Woodland

In the woods where the squirrels play,
A raccoon sneezed and scared away.
The owls hoot, with giggles shared,
While mushrooms dance as they declared.

A bear wearing sneakers chased a gnome,
Who tried to outrun, far from his home.
The trees chuckle, leaves in a swirl,
In this forest where eyebrows unfurl.

An otter slipped on a mossy stone,
In the water he splashed, then groaned and moaned.
Frogs croaked laughter as they jumped about,
In this jolly place, there's never a doubt.

So join the fun, let spirits rise,
In this woodland of laughter, a grand surprise.
Nature's playground of whimsy sown,
Where everything's funny when you're not alone.

Echoes of the Enchanted Path

On a path where the shadows linger,
A rabbit flips with a twitching finger.
A hedgehog sings in a funny tune,
While butterflies dance like little balloons.

The paths are dotted with giggles bright,
As critters plot mischief through the night.
A fox tells tales of a chicken's scheme,
While crickets send messages through a beam.

The owl spins wisdom, but with a jest,
Advice so silly, it's hard to digest.
But laughter echoes under the full moon,
Where every step feels like a cartoon.

So wander here, where laughter flows,
In forests bright, where anything glows.
On this enchanted path, joy will not part,
Where every creature has a funny heart.

Secrets Beneath the Canopy

Beneath the leaves, where shadows creep,
A gopher tripped, went down with a leap.
With acorns tumbling all around,
Acorn caps bounced without a sound.

A wise old turtle jested and teased,
While a cheeky parrot squawked, 'Please!'
Fungi chuckle in spots of delight,
As raccoons plan mischief every night.

The wind whispers secrets, full of quirks,
About frogs in top hats, playing their works.
While chipmunks spin tales of nuts and cheese,
In this lively realm with laughter that frees.

So come and explore, where wonders combine,
With silliness woven in every line.
Secrets dwell where the critters boast,
In this canopy laughter reigns the most.

The Forest's Heartbeat

The forest beats with a merry thrum,
With trees that giggle and critters that hum.
A chipmunk jives, doing a twirl,
While a fox in a bowtie gives a whirl.

The brook's aquartet, splashing in tune,
As frogs join in under the silver moon.
A pine cone fell, causing a ruckus,
While mice played chess, it tickled their focus.

An owl said, 'Whooo!' in laughter and grace,
As squirrels held a nutty race.
Each heartbeat echoes a symphony grand,
Where joy in the forest is perfectly planned.

So wander the trails where fun takes the lead,
In this lively place, laughter is the creed.
The forest's heartbeat sings sweet and clear,
With creatures that smile, inviting you near.

The Dance of the Forest Shadows

In the woods where shadows prance,
Squirrels twirl a little dance.
Rabbits hop and then they stare,
Wondering if they should join there.

A raccoon leads with jingling bells,
While owls laugh from their secret wells.
The trees sway with a breeze so light,
As moonbeams paint the scene at night.

Frogs croak loudly, join the beat,
While fireflies buzz and blink their greet.
The forest hosts a grand charade,
Of furry friends in a masquerade.

But when dawn breaks, they scatter quick,
Back to their homes, the woods' little tricks.
Who knew they hid such glee and cheer?
In the forest, it's mischief that's dear!

Legends Beneath the Leafy Boughs

Underneath the leafy haze,
Frogs tell stories of silly ways.
The chipmunk claims he once could fly,
While a beetle rolls its eyes nearby.

A tale of giants sprouting wings,
And foxes flaunting diamond rings.
The laughter echoes through the trees,
As critters chuckle with a tease.

Down by the brook, the frogs unite,
With plans to prank the owls at night.
A bucket of nuts, a wild scheme,
In the forest, they plot and dream.

But when the sun shows its bright face,
They scurry back to their secret place.
Legends swirl like autumn leaves,
In funny whispers, the forest weaves!

Secrets of the Sylvan Path

On the sylvan path where shadows play,
Squirrels gossip about their day.
A wise old owl gives a crooked grin,
As a funny tale is about to begin.

The deer discuss their grass buffet,
And how it grows in a quirky way.
The bees buzz by, in search of fun,
While mischief waits for everyone.

A hedgehog tells of a prickly plight,
When he lost his way in the moonlight.
With giggles shared among the crowd,
Nature's secrets are whispered loud.

As dusk approaches, they yearn to run,
Creating chaos, oh what fun!
With each secret shared, a laugh is gained,
In the woodland where humor is unchained!

Starlit Stories of the Wilderness

When night descends, stars burst with glee,
The wildlife gather for a spree.
A raccoon regales with tales of snacks,
While rabbits plot a flee-from-packs.

The wise old tortoise thinks he's cool,
Debating if speed is a silly rule.
As owls hoot their wise remarks,
The fireflies light up the dark parks.

A coyote howls with humorous flair,
While crickets chirp without a care.
The bunnies giggle at their own fluff,
Claiming they're tough, while acting all gruff.

But soon they yawn, the laughter wanes,
Under the stars, they share their claims.
In wilderness, each night's a thrill,
With starlit stories, they love to fill!

Glimpses of Glory in Green

In a forest so bright, with trees tall and proud,
Squirrels plot mischief beneath a green shroud.
A bird sings a tune, but it's slightly off-key,
While frogs in a chorus croak wildly in glee.

A raccoon with style wears a hat made of leaves,
He twirls with a wink, causing quite a few thieves.
The laughter erupts from the branches above,
As critters unite in a dance full of love.

The shadows stretch long as the sun starts to fade,
Each critter concocts its own grand charade.
The deer form a line in a serious parade,
But trip on a root, oh, what a charade!

All end with a giggle, as night starts to creep,
The forest may tire, but it never can sleep.
For whispers and chuckles from far undergrowth,
Speak of blessed adventures and nature's great oath.

The Bastion of the Beech

A beech tree stands firm, with a grin on its bark,
It knows all the gossip that's made after dark.
With acorns for ammo, a squirrel on high,
Declares this is war 'gainst the birds in the sky.

The beetles convene in a council so grand,
Debating the odds of a hedgehog's demand.
They wager on who'll steal food from the pile,
While a tortoise nods and grins with a smile.

A rabbit named Pete donned a coat made of fluff,
Declared with a shout, that he'd had quite enough!
"Let's party tonight!" he proclaimed to the crew,
While the others agreed, saying, "What else can we do?"

So the beech hosted dances, with roots as the floor,
And everyone chimed in with laughter galore.
The stars watched in wonder, as grasshoppers played,
Swinging to beats that the owls serenade.

Fables on the Forest Floor

Beneath all the boughs where the shadows can stretch,
There lies a fine tale that moss will etch.
A worm named Lars thought he'd take a grand trip,
Only to find he'd slipped on a slip!

A spider, quite charming, spun webs made of dreams,
Caught thoughts of the squirrels in bright silver beams.
She offered them visions of world's whirling dance,
But they just took a sprout and started to prance.

A lizard in sunglasses lounged near a stone,
Sighed, "Life's pretty sweet, but I'm often alone."
He cracked open a nut, offered some to a bee,
Who buzzed back a grin, "Let's both drink some tea!"

Soon all were invited, the forest alive,
What started as fables made everybody thrive.
With stories and laughter, this gathering soared,
On the forest floor, every heart was restored.

Sketches from the Silenced Glen

In a glen where the silence holds whispers so tight,
A hedgehog named Lou brought a comic delight.
With tales of his travels and snacks on the way,
He made all the creatures laugh hard every day.

A turtle named Tilly joined in with a joke,
"Why don't we race?!" made the whole glen choke.
While the rabbit shot by, with a twinkle and hop,
The laughter erupted and just wouldn't stop.

At dusk when all seemed to quietly land,
Fireflies flickered, with their lights like a band.
The critters held hands and began a soft hum,
They knew every giggle would keep the night warm.

With sketches of mischief that played on each face,
The glen turned to magic, a make-believe space.
And though time would tick, as it often does here,
The joy traveled through, in each crackling cheer.

The Lore of the Leafy Lanes

In leafy lanes where tempers flare,
A squirrel stole my sandwich, beware!
It danced around with quite the flair,
Chasing it was like running in air.

The owls hoot jokes that never land,
While raccoons form a rock band,
They sing of snacks and food unplanned,
And leave me with a taste so bland.

A rabbit once wore my favorite hat,
It claimed it was a fashion spat,
With ears so long and a stylish spat,
I learned to never argue with a vat.

Now every stroll brings laughter bright,
In leafy lanes under moonlight,
With critters dancing in plain sight,
Who knew nature could be so light!

Underneath the Arbor's Embrace

Underneath the branches wide,
A gopher tried to take me for a ride,
It said, "Hop on, there's nothing to hide!"
Yet all it offered was dirt and pride.

A parrot squawked in accents bold,
Telling jokes from days of old,
With punchlines that were purest gold,
But left me feeling rather cold.

The leaves were giggling at my shoe,
As if they knew what I would do,
Tripped by roots, my balance flew,
And laughter filled the morning dew.

Beneath this bough, the tales unfold,
Of jesters sneezing and treasures sold,
A world where every day is gold,
And fun is worth its weight in bold!

Saga of the Silent Streams

Along the banks of whispered streams,
A fish told jokes that burst like dreams,
With fins that flapped in giddy schemes,
    It had me laughing at its themes.

The frogs croaked out their funny tunes,
While turtles shuffled through the dunes,
    Holding court like little loons,
Wearing hats made of spoons and moons.

Each ripple brought a splash of cheer,
With minnows wiggling near and dear,
They twirled around, without a fear,
Creating laughter we could all hear.

So join the dance by the babbling run,
Where every glance means more fun begun,
    The tale of streams is never done,
With glee and giggles for everyone!

The Green Enchantment

In the forest green, a magic spun,
Where bushes danced just for fun,
A beetle rapped, oh what a pun!
It jived to rhythms, no need to run.

The mushrooms teamed in cap and gown,
Pretending to be the talk of the town,
They cackled on as I walked down,
In their grand ball, I wore a frown.

A deer once tried to play charades,
Using leaves in funny cascades,
But I just stood there, lost in shades,
While laughter bubbled like summer parades.

So here in the green where the humor grows,
With all the critters putting on shows,
The enchantment of nature, as everyone knows,
Is a giggle-filled journey wherever one goes!

Heartbeats of the Ancient Oak

Old oak stood proud and tall,
With a bark that winked at all.
Squirrels danced in a playful race,
Telling tales of their nutty grace.

Branches creaked with every sigh,
'Who needs a gym?' the squirrels cry.
While birds in nests had quite the show,
Debating on how fast they could go.

The shade above played hide and seek,
While rabbits plotted their next sneak.
Under the watch of a crow so wise,
Who feigned a yawn, rolled sleepy eyes.

As sunset fell, colors swirled,
Our oak still swayed, unfurled.
Laughter echoed through the glade,
While bushes blushed, unafraid.

The Path Less Taken

Two trails forked beneath a tree,
One was straight, clear as can be.
The other danced in twists and turns,
Where laughter lived and mischief yearns.

With boots of mud and hats of leaves,
Travelers walked like playful thieves.
Chasing shadows, no time to trip,
As birds above took inventory of the quip.

A bee buzzed near with a knowing glance,
While ants below formed quite a dance.
They argued hard, who'd lead the way,
"I'm busier!" one little ant did say.

Thus, they stumbled, but no one fell,
With giggles heard where laughter dwells.
The path less taken, a bowl of fun,
With every step, a story spun.

The Symphony of the Swaying Cedars

In a grove where cedars sway,
Wind tickled leaves in a playful way.
Boughs harmonized with a rustling sound,
While squirrels drummed on the ground.

A fox, flamboyant, pranced along,
Pawing the notes to an old folk song.
The raccoons clapped in furry delight,
Under a sky painted lavender light.

The cedars laughed, their roots deep set,
With giggles shared, a true duet.
Nature's jesters, performers in line,
Creating mischief, oh so divine!

The sun dipped low, a curtain call,
Where shadows danced, and night became tall.
And thus, the trees, in whispered tones,
Bore witness to the night's croons and moans.

Echoing Footsteps on Mossy Ground

Footsteps echoed, soft and light,
On mossy floors, a funny sight.
Giggles bounced from tree to tree,
As creatures played hide and seek with glee.

A hedgehog spun in a leafy ball,
While a tortoise took a leisurely crawl.
The soundtrack? A chorus of chirps and squeaks,
From frogs and owls who played for weeks.

Each step a dance on nature's stage,
With antics that could fill a page.
A bear sneezed, causing all to freeze,
As butterflies twirled with utmost ease.

In this world where laughter grows,
And friendships blossom as nature shows.
The echoing footsteps, a playful tease,
In the heart of woods, where joy's a breeze.

Secrets in the Sap

In the woodlands, whispers play,
Squirrels giggle all the day.
Sticky sap on paws and nose,
Oh what fun, the mischief grows!

Trees shuffle leaves like silly hats,
Barking dogs and chattering rats.
Acorn parties every night,
Under stars, all feels just right!

Bumbles bees join in the dance,
With buzzing tunes, they take a chance.
The forest winks, the flowers shout,
What a raucous, lively bout!

In each crevice, giggles hide,
Nature's joy can't be denied.
Come join the fun beneath the green,
Where secrets live, and laughter's seen!

The Lightness of Leaf and Limb

Leafy dancers in the breeze,
Swinging low with perfect ease.
Branches bend and twirl around,
Nature's circus, joy profound!

A clumsy bird, it takes to flight,
A tumble here, a flap just right.
The sun reflects on laughing streams,
Where nothing's ever as it seems.

Frogs don tuxedos, jump with flair,
Mice with capes flow through the air.
The bigger creatures scratch their heads,
While tiny critters dance in spreads.

It's a riot in soft, crisp air,
Each step a giggle, light as prayer.
In the woods, all worries cease,
Where joy abounds and laughter's peace!

Burdened by the Beauty

Oh the bloom that graces hills,
Dancing wild with wondrous thrills.
Fluffy clouds wear silly frowns,
As butterflies roam in their gowns.

The flowers sing a lively tune,
While raccoons play beneath the moon.
Each petal sighs, a heavy load,
Yet joy erupts along the road!

A hedgehog ponders life so grand,
With prickly thoughts, he takes a stand.
In every fern, a story spins,
The laughter builds on wooded whims.

Covered in blooms—what a sight!
The scene, a bloom of pure delight.
Nature chuckles, a heavy heart,
Yet lightness flows like fine art!

Unseen Paths of the Pine

Underneath the pine's embrace,
Lies a world full of wild grace.
Chipmunks dart with cheeky glee,
Finding acorns, just you see!

Paths of laughter twist and turn,
With every step, new joys we learn.
Pine needles whisper silly stuff,
Encouraging all when times get tough!

The fox in boots struts with pride,
While bunnies hop in quickened stride.
Each shadow holds a playful tease,
Where pine trees sway, their spirits please.

So step on in, don't be shy,
Adventure awaits, oh me, oh my!
In unseen paths, we twine and play,
Laughing through our woodland way!

www.ingramcontent.com/pod-product-compliance
Lightning Source LLC
Chambersburg PA
CBHW072142200426
43209CB00051B/257